TREASURES OF SPANISH PAINTINGS

TEXT: **M. WIESENTHAL**
DESING: **F. SUBARROCA**
ICHONOGRAPHY: **SALMER**

1st. Edition, March 1979
I.S.B.N.
84-7424-074-3

INTRODUCTION

There are few countries that can boast such a dazzling succession of painters as Spain: Juan de Juanes, Ribera, Morales, Velázquez, Murillo, Goya... Even when Spain is economically and physically in a state of crisis, geniuses have tended to emerge, as if to say that the Spanish are destined to be delivered from these dark moments by the light of the plastic arts, and their strength of expression. Goya's works are the most often quoted as examples of that dramatic struggle of the Spanish in the face of difficulty. Velázquez and Zurbarán in their turn, in portrait and still-life, pursued the very essence of life. Spanish genius always seeks a definite image of things, defining profile, surface and line. When his country began to travel in the roads of misery and decadence, the Spaniard pulled out his brushes and drew, almost savagely, the desolate scene around him: the dwarf's deformed body, the haughty profile of the bourgeois, the simplicity of clay... The artist is redeemed by this close contact with reality. Close to the earth, the artist becomes human; faced with a dwarf or a tramp, painting is transformed into meditation and criticism.

But in Spain painting has never been an exclusively national resource, for great artists like Rubens and El Greco, though born abroad, worked in Spain where they found refuge and patronage. The Spanish sovereigns were lovers of painting; indeed the Prado Museum itself must be considered as an exclusive royal foundation, whose art collection was the continued effort of many sovereigns. This royal influence has at times dictated the direction of Spanish painting. Thus, Velázquez never portrayed the great bankers and businessmen who were the typical sitters of Rembrandt and other European masters. Spanish artists frequently and without hesitation, change their themes from royal and religious, to the humble everyday scene. This is the reason why when a king or a saint is portrayed, the commoner or even the thief underlying the noble costume is always brought out. And when the sitter is a jester or a pauper, the holy man and the king seem to be latent even in this portrait of poverty.

Within the general history of art, the personality of Spanish painting is quite distinct. Spanish artists traveled to Europe, mainly to Italy, to get better acquainted with classical art and make contact with the different schools and tendencies of their time. But the best works of Spanish painting have originated from the country's own life, and are depictions of its people and geography, portraying the drama of its history: Goya's executions; Zurbarán's monks and still lives; Velázquez's portraits... The painting of Spain is an explanation of its history and of the spirit of its people. To visit this great gallery of paintings is to discover the deepest secrets of Spanish life. There are peoples whose heart contains a philosophy, a melody or the step of a dance, and they feel happy only when reality resembles that philosophy, that melody or that step. Italians are happy when they sing; the Viennese find themselves when they dance; the Germans live their symphonies and the French are given to cogitation and philosophising... The Spaniard carries in his very soul the memory of some pictures, of certain colors, and certain expressions. When his life turns tragic, he wraps it up in the colors of his palette. One sometimes feels that the key episodes in the history of Spain, ranging from the discovery of half the world to modern revolutions, have been merely ingenious means of giving color to life.

ROMANESQUE PAINTERS

In the panorama of the Spanish Romanesque painting, one region stands out: Catalonia. Italian and Eastern influences first reached the Mediterranean coast, where they originated an artistic movement of great quality. Catalonian artists, mostly coming from a monastic environment, created one of the most academic schools of Romanesque painting. We should keep in mind that this is an art of narrow theological conceptions, specially in the realm of painting. Each decorative element is ordered and set within the whole, like a sentence in a prayer. At times the artist seems to place his figures outside time and space, remote from worldly cares; even ornaments are simple geometrical lines or curved ribbons. The churches in the Catalonian Pyrenees still exhibit some of the most brilliant jewels of this schools, works that appear to have been painted by monks who were essentially illuminators of Bibles and other liturgical manuscripts. In this group of Pyreneic painting, mention must be made of the works of San Quirze de Pedret, San Miguel de Angulasters (Andorra), Santa Eulalia de Estahon, Esterri de Cardos, San Martín de Fenollar... The best work of this series is, however, the presbytery of San Clemente de Tahull, one of the most beautiful examples of medieval theological painting. Another masterpiece is the decoration of the church of Santa María de Tahull, dedicated to the *Theotocos,* the Mother of God, who is shown elegantly holding the infant Christ. Contemplating these stylized images of Tahull, one is reminded of the spiritual intensity later to be found in El Greco.

In documents of the Cathedral archives in Barcelona, appear the names of some painters of those times, such as Guillén, Berenguer and Bartolomé. A certain Johanes signs a 13th century altar hanging found in Lérida.

In the rest of Spain, specially in the Central plateau, a noteworthy artistic movement grew up in late medieval times, but the frescoes have not come down

Altar hanging of Bohi, Museum of Art of Catalonia, Barcelona.

Altar hanging of Avia, Museum of Art of Catalonia, Barcelona.

to us in good conditions. One of the most beautiful works here is that of the San Baudilio de Berlanga in Soria. The artist of San Baudilio was probably a layman who did not obey as strictly as the Catalonian monks the Byzantine rules of painting, and his work is freer and more imaginative.

In the province of Segovia we find the hermitage of Veracruz, on the edge of the ancient village of Maderuelo. Its decoration is very simple, and the hieratic figures are reminiscent of the Catalonian style.

We also find a clear Byzantine influence in the works at San Isidoro de Leon, whose marthex gathers together some of the most important Romanesque paintings in Europe. The painters of San Isidoro undoubtedly knew Eastern art through miniatures. The Catalonian Romanesque has also given us,

besides frescoes decorating churches, a superb collection of panels which were placed as decorative pieces on the altars. Some of these masterpieces are preserved in the Museum of Vich.

PEDRO BERRUGUETE

Pedro Berruguete, born in Palencia, lived for a time in Italy where he worked on the decoration of the Duke of Urbino's palace. In Castille he probably became acquainted with the Flemish artists of the school of Van Eyck. His works display this strong nordic influence, enlivened by the colorful art of Italy. He is the most representative painter of the Spain of the Catholic kings, and can be considered as a faithful reporter of everyday life in the 15th century. He also painted several altar pieces with religious

themes, including the magnificent Annunciation in the Cartuja of Miraflores, where the full power of his palette is seen. His most famous work is the Auto-da-fé, kept in the Museum of El Prado, depicting the story of the heresiarch Ramón who was saved from death by Santo Domingo (St. Dominic). His work is the epitome of delicacy, aristocratic sensibility and deep contemplation.

VELAZQUEZ

The life of Diego de Silva y Velázquez is, like his work, a wonderful synthesis of nature and art. He walks the earth like the great chosen ones, like a Leonardo or a Goethe, finding everywhere the perfect environment for the ripening of his genius. His birth into the nobility and his years as an apprentice already give evidence of this mysterious gift that will turn him into a great painter. The son of a noble Portuguese family that emigrated from Oporto to Seville, his noble lineage gave him entry to the court and provided him with a unique perspective over the aristocracy. He was educated in Seville where

HONORIVS TERTIƲ

ORDINÊ COFIRMAVIT

UNUS BAPT
DOMI ISMA
NUS AD
UNA EPHE
FIDES SIOS
UNUM 4.CAP°

Cristobal Llorens, Judicial Book Trial, Museum of Fine Arts, Valencia.

Berruguete, St. Dominic de Guzmán presiding over an Auto-da-fe, The Prado, Madrid.

Velázquez, The Spinners, The Prado, Madrid.

Velázquez, Self-Portrait, Museum of Fine Arts, Valencia.

he felt the influence of Pacheco as well as of the great Andalusian artistic tradition. Marrying his teacher's daughter, he later acquired the protection of the powerful Count-Duke of Olivares, an Andalusian aristocrat who gained Velázquez entry into the court. Once appointed royal painter in Madrid, he had free access to the magnificent private collections of the king, and was able to make a detailed study of Italian painting. He also met Rubens, who initiated him into the secrets of his exuberant and cultivated technique. Velázquez's biography is lacking in unusual or exaggerated detail. He lived a quiet and unworried life, without those romantic indulgments that many

common critics always want to see in geniuses. His spiritual life allowed him to observe reality with an original vision, without stress, pain or lies. This is why he is a genuine painter of reality, depicting objects as almost biologically alive, in their natural atmosphere, with their natural colors. His position as royal painter obliged him to dedicate himself exclusively to portrait painting. In this field he stands out as a real humanist, with the peculiar gift of being able to portray his models without distorting their features. It could well be said that when he paints man he dignifies and elevates him.

Under royal commission, Velázquez traveled several

Velázquez, The Topers, The Prado, Madrid.

Velázquez, Philip IV, The Prado, Madrid.

times to Italy and got to know in detail the works of the Renaissance masters. He became a personal friend of Ambrosio Spinola, captain of the Spanish infantry regiments, who was to be immortalized in his famous painting of the "Rendición de Breda." He also painted the portraits of his first patron, the Count-Duke of Olivares, and of the Royal family. In his first period he enjoyed popular themes, but he always contrasts his prosaic figures with the lyrical backgrounds and distant landscapes. As a knight of the order of St. James he portrayed himself in the renowned picture of "Las Meninas." This is probably the painting in which Velázquez has most deeply expressed his sense of space and the mystery of time. His characters seem to have entered into the vibrant atmosphere of another world, where things acquire different contour and expression. "He was able to

paint what cannot be seen," said Jovellanos. We know that the Infanta Isabel de Velasco died soon after Velázquez painted her, and seeing this painting we feel as if the artist had guessed this simply looking at reality with his penetrating eyes. Velázquez is beyond a doubt, the painter of reality. But real things, like human faces, are transformed under his gaze into profound mystery. He was an untiring worker and would retouch his paintings even after the death of his models, changing a fold here, moving the position of a hand there. His brush is, however, full of life and inspiration. He mastered all the tones of gray to make shadows softer and to give depth to his spaces. His lights are never sharp, but seem to caress the skin of his models. It has often been said that he is the genius of realistic painting, but for him life is live energy, the same power that

Velázquez, *Queen Elizabeth of France, wife of Philip IV*, The Prado, Madrid.

Velázquez, *Don Gaspar de Guzmán, Count-Duke of Olivares*, The Prado, Madrid.

Velázquez, *The God Mars*, The Prado, Madrid.

drew the stars out of the darkness, that created life, and vibrates in the heart of man.

EL GRECO

Domenicus Theotocapoulos, known as El Greco, was born In Candia, on the island of Crete in 1541. Those ancient lands of the classical Mediterranean were then under the control of Venice and the young Greek was thus enabled, in 1560, to move to Italy. In the pleasant city of the canals he became familiar with the works of Tintoretto Bassano, and also was a disciple of Tiziano. This learning did not leave any deep impression on his style, for his own temperament was not akin to the sumptuous coloring of the Venice school. El Greco was an intense temperament of realistic vision, but with a mystical mind and frigid manners. He would finally find in Spain, after 1576, the best atmosphere for his genius to ripen. He probably came to Spain attracted by the art collection of the Escorial, and settled in Toledo where he lived until his death. Today he is widely known as a Spanish painter, identified with the soul

▷

of Toledo, as a silent witness of the decadence of the Empire.

He was known as a quiet and cultivated introvert. With the benefits of his paintings he was able to afford a luxurious and refined life. He lived like a Spanish nobleman of his time, never heeding tomorrow, leaving behind few estates and various debts. From the remains of his private library we know that he was an eager reader of Homer and the Bible, and was also sculptor and architect and a neo-Platonist. His art reflects the aesthetic Byzantine influence in the hierarchtic pose of his figures as well

*Velázquez,
The Jester
Calabazas,
The Prado,
Madrid.*

*Velázquez,
Christ on the
Cross, The
Prado, Madrid.*

El Greco, Baptism of Christ, The Prado, Madrid.

as in the vertical deformation of his models.
El Greco captures, with a natural instinct, the pathetic feeling of Spanish history; he observes reality with a slight meditative sadness, and his bodies have death-like colors, as if only inner life existed in them. In Toledo he painted several religious works (The Spoliation, the Assumption, the Annunciation, St. Francis of Assisi, etc.), and also portrayed several important figures at the court of Philip II; faces and hands appear in his works as patches of light in the midst of a dark background. This is the vision of a Spain that was being disintegrated and consumed by darkness. El Greco was the great painter of Toledo, no one like him has seen the city surrounded by an aura of angels. The earthy colors of Toledo resemble those of the skin of his models.

His masterpiece, one of the most remarkable works is the history of painting, is the Burial of Count of Orgaz, preserved in the small Toledan church of Santo Tomé. The origin of this work is an ancient legend which says that St. Esteban and St. Agustin descended from heaven to bury with their own hands the Conde de Orgaz, a mirror of Christian virtues. Using this humble subject matter, El Greco was able to give supreme expression to his genius, creating a true spiritual symphony with the enigma of death as a background. In order to understand El Greco we have to penetrate the mysteries of the Apocalypse. His work is the art of Doomsday, when heaven is shattered and man's eyes are dazzled by the blinding light of the Infinite.

GOYA

Son of a master gilder, and descended from a well-to-do provincial family, Francisco Goya was born in 1746 in the small Aragonese town of Fuendetodos. He tried to learn the basic principles of his art in the workshop of José Luzán, but his control of technique would always be deficient in the eyes of the strict teachers of his time. He moved to Naples to complete his studies and here he made his first bid for success as an academic painter. Protected by his friend, the painter Francisco Bayeu, who later became

El Greco, Portrait of a Gentleman, The Prado, Madrid.

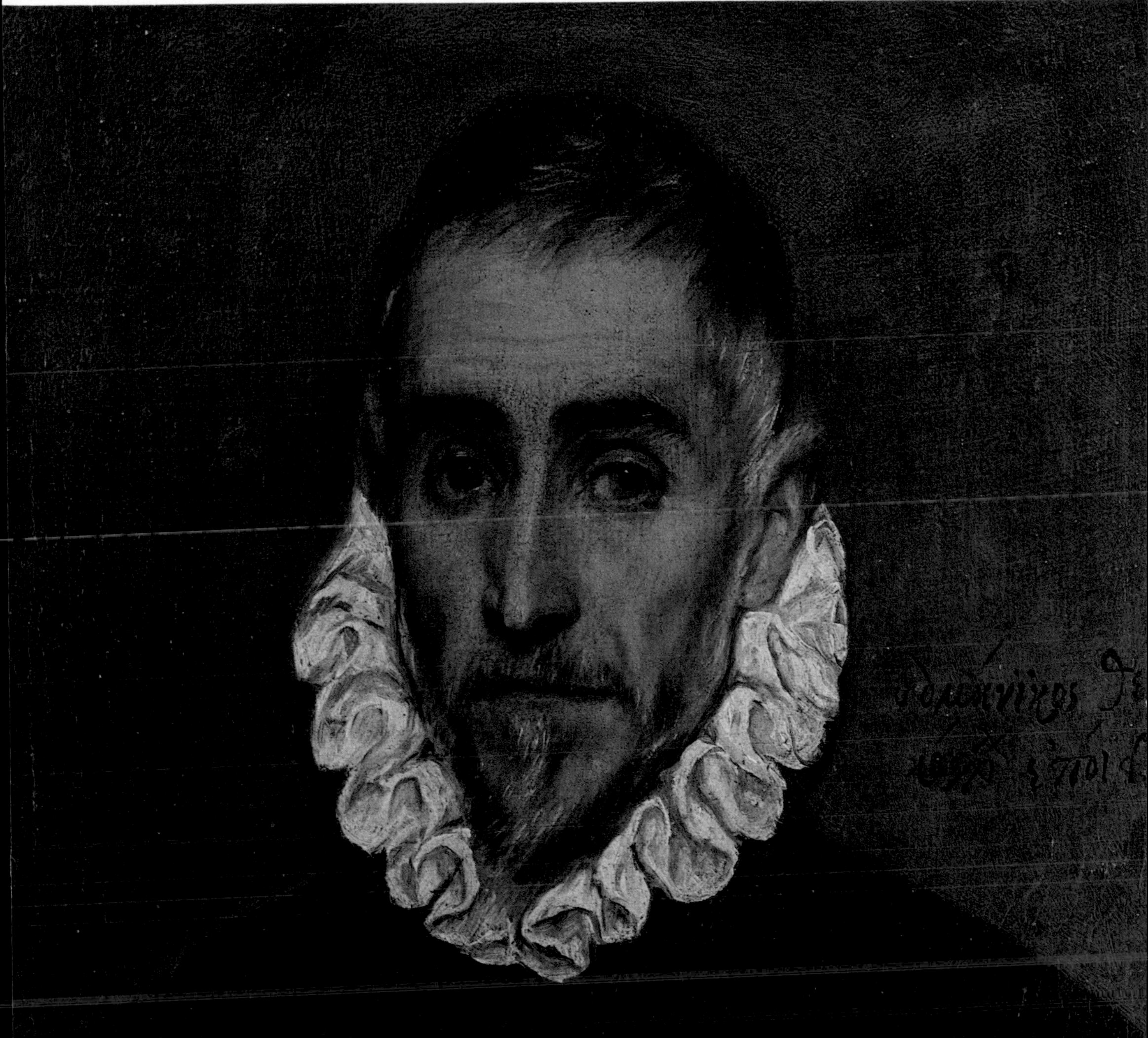

El Greco, Portrait of a Nobleman with Hand on Breast, The Prado, Madrid.

El Greco, St. Francis, The Prado, Madrid.

El Greco,
St. John the
Evangelist,
The Prado,
Madrid.

El Greco,
Christ carrying
the Cross,
The Prado,
Madrid.

El Greco,
The Burial
of Count
Orgaz, The
Prado, Madrid.

El Greco,
St. Andrew
and St.
Francis, The
Prado, Madrid.

El Greco,
The Holy
Family,
Hospital of
Tavera,
Toledo. ▷

El Greco,
St. Francis
Praying,
Museum of
Fine Arts,
Valencia. ▷

Goya, The Marriage, The Prado, Madrid.

Goya, Self-Portrait, The Prado, Madrid.

his father-in-law, he won the contract for the decoration of the church of the Pilar in Zaragoza. Still under the patronage of Bayeu, he later moved to Madrid where he painted several cartoons for the royal tapestry works of Santa Bárbara. In 1780, continuing in this academic style, he was appointed as the king's painter. In court he had occasion to study the great royal collections and soon became the most incisive portrait painter of his time. This is perhaps, one of the most balanced, happiest periods of his career, his genius is already apparent but emerges with great simplicity, and even with a certain human tenderness. In 1792 he falls seriously ill becoming deaf as he was to remain until the end of his life. From this time come the famous "Caprichos," (Caprices) that reveal the nightmares and afflictions of his soul, torn between the rationalism of the 18th century and the irrational fantasies of the 19th century.

Goya is the archetype of the Spanish bourgeois of his time: unrefined, betrayed by the plebeian environment of a decaying country, and pursued by a demanding and fanatical elite. In this atmosphere a painter like Velázquez would not have been able to grow and mature. The painter of this era had to be a Goya, genius, temperamental, pathetic, and sick. At times the desperate Goya looks for redemption in the street, in popular fiestas and in the villainous or picaresque figures that roamed the popular neighborhoods of Madrid. After such excursions, however, he immediately returns to his own fantasies, to his illustrations, to those romantic and crooked figures which seem to anticipate the Quasimodo of Notre Dame. When Napoleon's troops invaded the country he felt the suffering of Spain acutely, and painted the dramatic "Executions."

◁ *El Greco, St. John the Baptist, Museum of Fine Arts, Valencia. The Pentecost. The Annunciation. The Prado. Madrid.*

When Ferdinand VIII returned to Spain in 1814, Goya found himself in a virtually untenable position. Being a man of authentic and sincere temperament, he fought against both sides: against the French atrocities and against the fanatical excesses of the absolutist repression. Persecuted by the king's secret police, he again took shelter in his work and began to etch the superb series of the "Desastres de la Guerra," a fierce protest of the artist who had once· believed in the victory of reason over the brute force of violence. He mastered the etching and burin techniques as no one had done before. But he had already fallen into the net of obsession. He decorated the walls of his house on the banks of the Manzanares

Goya, Ferdinand VII, The Prado, Madrid.

Goya, Charles IV, The Prado, Madrid.

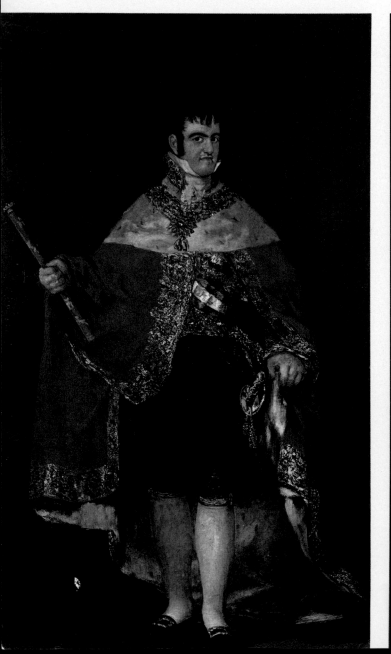

Goya, The Royal Family of Charles IV, The Prado, Madrid.

"the deaf man's house," as it was called, with the famous black paintings that are like a desperate scream, an incurable illness, a protest from a deaf man to all those other deaf people around him. Goya was above all a man of sincerity, a dedicated worker and a genius towering over those times of affliction and misfortune. His sensibility, like his health, broke in that environment of tragedy which prophesied all the excesses of the Romanticism. In his moments of sanity as a portrait painter he gave us works more critical and acutely sensitive than his own Caprices, but these paintings express a hopeless serenity, that impossible tenderness, and a lost sense of beauty. After him was to come the deluge of Romanticism, the age of excess, of the monsters and caricatures. The superficial romantic view of Goya, through eyes unaccostumed to pain, was to lead painting over facile paths of fever and protest. But Goya's message is deeper, more genuine. He deforms shapes with his obsession, and renews our belief in reality.

In 1824 Goya moved to France to escape the

Goya, *The Dukes of Osuna and Their Children*, The Prado, Madrid. ▷

Goya, *Doña Tadea Arias de Enríquez*, The Prado, Madrid.

Goya, *Queen Maria Louisa*, The Prado, Madrid.

Goya, The Clothed Maja (detail), The Prado, Madrid.

Goya, Bullfight Scene, The Prado, Madrid.

consequences of absolutist repression. He died in
Bordeaux in 1828, exiled and alone, knowing that
his critics and disciples would betray his work.

MURILLO

Bartolomé Esteban Murillo was born in Seville in
1618. Although some biographers claim that he
traveled far from the Andalusian capital, most of

his life was spent in his native city. He was a simple
man, of humble ancestry, who studied his craft
with dedication. He started by painting pictures in
series for the Andalusian fairs and for export to the
New World, thus acquiring that smoothness
of style that is seen in all his work. Zurbarán
influenced his style, but Murillo's own misticism
came from more optimistic sources, from a more
delicate and feminine sensibility. His religiosity was
not a product of the convent or the cloister. His

Goya, The Snowfall, The Prado, Madrid.

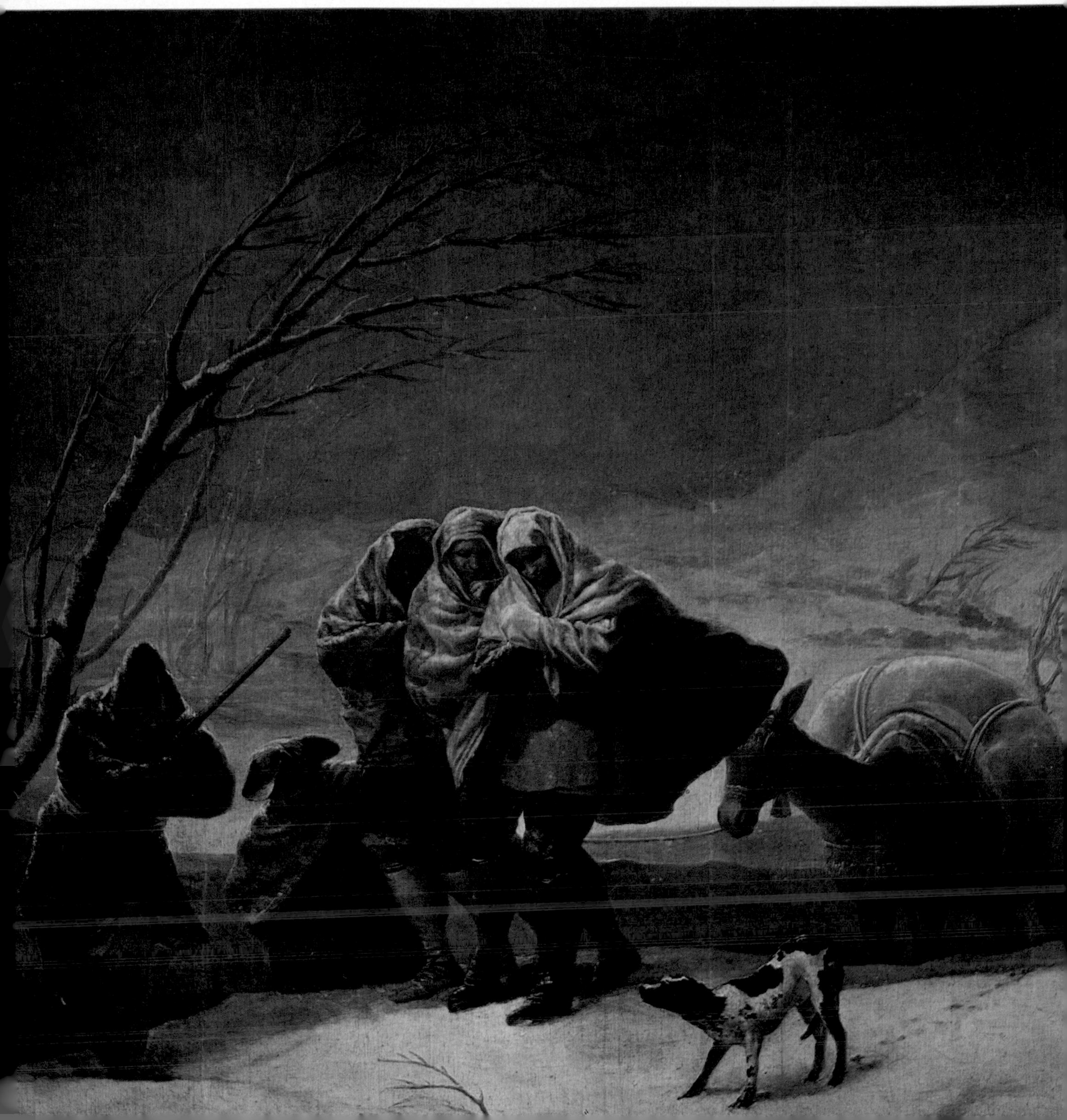

Goya, *The Burial of the Sardine, Real Academia de San Fernando, Madrid.*

Goya, *The 2nd of May, 1808, Madrid: The Charge of the Mamelukes, The Prado, Madrid.*

models come from the streets, lit by the sun that shines on the Sevillan squares.

Murillo is a misunderstood painter. It has been said that he is a minor artist, subject to the limitations of Andalusian piety. His work, however, stands for the trascendental revolution that took place in Spanish painting in the 18th century. The harmony of his compositions and the silken tonality of his palette reminds us of the European Baroque. He surrounds his figures by soft shadows, following Van Dyck's tradition and the Italian masters of his time.

The art of Murillo is born of that optimism that belongs to the popular Andalusian soul. This is not an intelectual religious feeling but rather an instinctive love for the beauty of Creation. Like the music of Mozart, his art seems to be directed by a spontaneous and naive rhythm. His brush always smiles, contrasts are softened and angles are melted into curves.

He worked mainly for the convents in Seville and the greatest part of his work is religious. Some of the greatest works were for the chapel of the Hospital de la Caridad, such as the San Juan de Dios carrying a sick man on his back, Moses striking the rock, the Multiplication of the loaves and fishes, etc. He painted a famous Immaculate Conception for the Hospital de Venerables Sacerdotes, later owned by Field Marshall Soult and now kept in the Prado. His Virgins made him famous and helped to create that false image of a naive painter, limited by popular sensibility.

It is said that he died falling from a scaffolding when he was working in the convent of the Capuchins in 1682, leaving unfinished the painting of the Betrothal of St. Catherine. Murillo is a painter with deep Spanish roots, but his aesthetic feeling is far distant from tenebrism or bitter realism. In him only the most optimistic tendencies of Spanish genius find expression. If El Greco and Zurbarán discovered the severe and tormented side of the Spanish soul, Murillo, gave painting a happy and feminine smile.

Goya, The Executions of 3rd May, 1808, on the Mountain of Prince Pio, The Prado, Madrid.

Goya, The Pilgrimage of San Isidro, The Prado, Madrid.

Goya, Saturn Devouring One of His Children, The Prado, Madrid.

Goya, Witches, Museum Lozano Galdiano, Madrid.

Goya, *The Witches' Sabbath, The Prado, Madrid.*

Goya. *Pilgrimage to the Fountains of San Isidro, The Prado, Madrid.*

Murillo, The Dream of the Patrician, Foundation of Santa Maria Maggiore of Rome, The Prado, Madrid.

CLAUDIO COELLO

Claudio Coello was born in Madrid in 1642, son of a Portuguese family that had settled in the capital of Philip IV. He studied in the studio of the painter Francisco Rizzi and probably traveled around Italy between 1656 and 1664. The influence of Italian art is decisive in his work. He painted religious themes for several Madrilenian churches; his masterpiece is "La Sagrada Forma," now kept in the sacristy of the Escorial. In this work, Coello appears to us not only as a great master, but also as the heir of the Renaissance Italian art.

He was greatly appreciated in the court, being the king's painter, and made portraits of several important figures of his time.

JUAN DE JUANES

Vicente Juan Maçip, known as Juan de Juanes, is one of the most remarkable painters of the Spanish Renaissance. His father, Vicente Maçip, introduced him to the secrets of the art of painting and to the Italian aesthetic canons. Juan de Juanes was educated in Valencia and there he received all the influence of light and color essential to the Mediterranean tradition. His work, in some respects, shows traces of medieval forms; but his perspective and color harmony define him as a Renaissance artist and disciple of Raphael. Most of his paintings are of religious themes (Scenes from the life of St. Esteban, the Last Supper, the Holy Family, etc.).

PEDRO DE MOYA

Pedro de Moya, of Granada (1610-1666), spent some
time as a soldier in Flanders, where he was able to
study the great painters of that country. He also lived
in England and for six months worked with
Van Dyck. In 1646 he returned to Granada where
he became famous as a painter of religious themes
(Apparition of the Virgin, the Birth, the Virgin and
the Boy crowning St. Magdalene of Pazzi, etc.).
His familiarity with the great European masters
helped him to give life to the Andalusian painting
of his time.

CREDITE
O GOTHI
CONSVBS
TANTIALEM
PATRI

*Murillo, The
Immaculate of
Soult, The Prado,
Madrid.*

*Murillo,
St. Thomas of
Villanueva,
Provincial
Museum of Fine
Arts, Seville.*

Murillo,
St. Anthony of
Padua.

Murillo, The
Vision of
St. Francis,
Provincial
Museum of Fine
Arts, Sevillle.

Murillo,
St. Ildefonso
Being
Rewarded by the
Virgin, The
Prado, Madrid.

JOSE DE RIBERA

Jusepe or José de Ribera was born near Valencia, in the city of Xativa which also produced the notorious Borgia family, who played an important role in the history of Italy. As a young man Ribera also moved to Italy, to study with the best masters of the time, Caravaggio and the Caraccis. Around 1616 he settled in Naples, which then belonged to the Spanish Crown, under the protection of the Viceroy. His compositions can stand side by side with those of the great Italian masters, but he kept his definitely Spanish liking for religious and popular themes, together with a pathetic feeling sometimes akin to grief. The undeniable Spanish feeling of his work was manifest in his nickname: "Lo

Claudio Coello, "La Sagrada Forma" Monastery of the Escorial, Madrid. *Juan de Juanes, The Last Supper, The Prado, Madrid.*

Spagnoletto." His work is characterized by impastos. He started painting in dark tones, attaining a greater lightness in his later works.

FRANCISCO BAYEU

The Aragonese Francisco Bayeu, Goya's father-in-law, was born in Zaragoza in 1734. He was the disciple of Luzán and Mengs. The decoration of the cathedral of El Pilar of Zaragoza and the cloister of Toledo were carried out by him. He was appointed painter of the king and also aided Goya. The latter gave us a famous portrait of him which can be seen in the Prado.

LUIS PARET Y ALCAZAR

Luis Paret is one of the greatest painters of the

Madrilenian school of the 18th century. He studied in Paris and Italy, where he perfected his refined style full of lyrism. His velvety colors and romantic sketches remind us of Watteau.

CARREÑO

The Asturian Juan Carreño, was born in Avilés in 1614, and settled in Madrid under the protection of Velázquez. He started to work with paintings of religious themes, but later, under the influence of Velázquez, he chose his teacher's same models, such as the jester Francisco Bazán, the dwarf Eugenia Martínez Vallejo, etc. He was a great portrait painter, with a firm and simple style, according to Spanish tradition, however, he incorporated into his work the movement and coloring that Rubens gave to the painting of his time.

Pedro de Moya, The Birth, Provincial Museum of Fine Arts, Seville.

Juan de Juanes, Don Luis de Castilla de Villanueva, The Prado, Madrid.

VALDES LEAL

Juan Valdés Leal, born in 1622, is one the most dramatic and interesting painters of the Sevillan school. He painted several pictures on religious themes for Andalusian monasteries. His two most striking works are the two pictures ordered by Don Miguel de Mañara, formerly Don Juan de Sevilla, that he painted for the church of the Hospital de la Caridad. In these astounding allegories, Valdés

José de Ribera, St. Paul the Hermit, The Prado, Madrid.

José de Ribera,
Archimedes, The
Prado, Madrid.

José de Ribera, *The Martyrdom of St. Bartholomew*, The Prado, Madrid.

Francisco Bayeu, The Prophesy of Isaiah, The Prado, Madrid.

Francisco Bayeu, The Promenade of Las Delicias in Madrid, The Prado, Madrid.

Leal expressed, quite pathetically, the mystery of death rising in victory over the corruption of the flesh and human vanity. His baroque techniques achieved spectacular dynamic effects by painting some parts of the picture out of focus.

LUCAS

Eugenio Lucas was born in Alcalá de Henares in 1824 and studied in the Academy of Fine Arts of San Fernando in Madrid. He was very soon attracted to Goya's style and captured with extraordinary facility the most intense of Goya's characteristics. With goyesque vehemence he painted his best bullfight scenes and famous

Luis Paret y
Alcázar,
Ferdinand VII
Taking the Oath
as Prince of
Asturias, The
Prado, Madrid.

Carreño de Miranda, Inés de Zúñiga, Museum Lázaro Galdiano, Madrid.

Carreño de Miranda, Charles II, The Prado, Madrid.

Inquisition pictures. As a painter he is relatively commonplace. The most original pieces of his work are his renowned ''Borrones'' (doodles), done with quill pen, which anticipate abstract art. His son Eugenio Lucas Villaamil was also a painter and continued his father's style.

ZURBARAN

Francisco de Zurbarán was born in the Extremaduran town of Fuen de Cantos, and most of his work was carried out in the ocher-colored lands of Andalusia and Extremadura. However, it would be risky to attribute to geography a decisive influence on Zurbarán's genius. His paintings stand out by his inner vision of man as an individual. His monks and saints are always depicted with singular realism, as people able to attain inner perfection without being unduly troubled by heavenly storms. The figures of El Greco are open to light, space and the open sky clouds. Zurbarán's

models, on the contrary, are locked in themselves appearing full of dignity. Even the saints depicted standing in heaven display a great terrestrial power, a firm gravitational force that makes then ''Children of man.'' It has been said of Zurbarán that he is a painter with great limitations of technique and imagination. But these same limitations constitute a large part of his originality. His realism touches us more today than any baroque bluff.

Zurbarán is the painter of the Counter Reformation, gloomy and pathetic, as well as faithful to the human condition. He feels an almost religious respect for reality and shapes. No one like him can depict monks' habits, dense fabrics, wool, etc. The Germans call ''Stilleben'' (life of silence) what Spanish call ''dead nature.'' The still lives of Zurbarán are not dead nature but vibration and living silence.

During his Sevillan period (1630-1639), Zurbarán painted his most important works. This was

when his forms acquired a greater solidity and
a greater serenity. Between 1638-39, he painted
the superb series in the Cartuja of Jerez de la
la Frontera, today distributed among the museums
of Cadiz, Grenoble and New York. From this time
also date the paintings of the Monastery
of Guadalupe, in which even the miracle becomes
a profoundly human phenomenom.
His last years were spent in Madrid in the most
absolute poverty, like one of the monks that he had
painted, almost fading away in front of the darkness
of the world.

VICENTE LOPEZ

Vicente López was born in Valencia in 1772,
and studied in Madrid with Maella. King
Ferdinand VII brought him to court and made him
his favorite portrait painter. López was a great
connoisseur of painting as well as a magnificent
draftsman, who worked his paintings over and over
again. He painted a splendid portrait of Goya, and it
is said that Goya, amazed by the quality of his
colleague's work, told him to stop working and that
he would instead give him some bullfighting lessons.
Goya was already too old to display such
spirits; but this anecdote is significant in that it tells
us about Vicente López painting. He decorated the
Charles II Hall in the Royal Palace of Madrid, and
made several religious pictures for Valencian
monasteries.
Some of his best works, together with the portrait
of Goya, are kept in the Prado, for instance

Zurbarán, The Friar Jerónimo Pérez, Real Academia de San Fernando, Madrid.

Zurbarán, Blessed Juan de Houghton, Provincial Museum of Fine Arts, Seville.

Zurbarán, The Vision of St. Pedro Nolasco, The Prado, Madrid.

Zurbarán, Hercules Scorched by the Centaur's Tunic. The Prado, Madrid.

Zurbarán, St. John the Evangelist, Provincial Museum of Fine Arts, Cádiz.

Valdes Leal, The Temptations of St. Jerome, Provincial Museum of Fine Arts, Seville.

Fernando VII, Queen Doña María Josefa Amalia, Queen Doña María Cristina de Borbón, Queen Isabel de Braganza and the Princess of Asturias.

VILLAVICENCIO

Pedro Núñez de Villavicencio was born in Seville in 1635. There he became a disciple of Murillo and

learnt much from his master. Carlos II was a keen admirer of his work and patronized him during his time in the court as portrait painter.

JOSE ELBO

The Andalusian José Elbo, born in Ubeda in 1802, was a disciple of José Aparicio. He drew delicate landscapes, portraits, and the bullfighting subjects that turned him into one of the most representative figures of his time.

MANUEL DE LA CRUZ

Manuel de la Cruz was born in Madrid in 1750. He made several works for the cloister of.
San Francisco el Grande, and a famous painting depicting the Fair of Madrid held in the Plaza de la Cebada.

RODRIGUEZ DE GUZMAN

The Sevillan Manuel Rodríguez de Guzmán, born in 1818, was a disciple of his fellow countryman José Domínguez Becquer. Some of his works were exhibited at the Universal Exhibition of Paris in 1855. He specialized in Andalusian genre scenes and was the painter par excellence of Andalusian fairs and pilgrimages.

FRANCISCO PACHECO

Francisco Pacheco was born in 1564, in Sanlúcar de Barrameda. The son of a family of sailors, he was a great humanist and a gifted connoisseur of the art of painting. He wrote a famous treatise, "Arte de la Pintura" (Art of Painting), as well as a worthy iconographical catalogue of the artists of his time, "Libro de verdaderos retratos" (Book of true portraits). He was the father-in-law of Velázquez and one of the key figures in the biography of this Spanish genius. As a painter he executed some works of remarkable realism, such as the "Scenes of the life of San Pedro Nolasco."

ANTONIO DE PEREDA

The Castilian Antonio de Pereda, born in Valladolid in 1608, was born into a family of artists. His upbringing undoubtedly aided his acquisition of discipline and technique. While deficient in the sobriety traditional to Spanish painting, he does

Vicente López, Charles IV, Museum of Fine Arts, Valencia.

display certain Flemish influences. He painted many religious works, as well as several fine still lives and original pictures of moral and allegoric themes.

MAZO

Juan Bautista Martínez del Mazo was born in Cuenca around the year 1612. He married a daughter of Velázquez and always lived under the shadow of the great master. His talent was first expressed in copying some pictures from the royal collections. His careful work as a copyist, opened his way to the secrets of the great masters of his time, specially Rubens and Jordaens. We find traces of his brush in some of the works from Velázquez's workshop. However, he lacks the sublime

skill of his master in creating distance between the model and the artist, and in depicting his models with absolute respect for reality. On the other hand, he gives his works a certain gentle touch that makes them light and graceful. It is probable that together with Velázquez, he painted the renowned hunting scene called ''La tela real'' (The royal cloth) that is on exhibition at the National Gallery in London. As a landscapist he created some remarkable pictures, blending techniques and poetic atmosphere: Vista de Zaragoza (View of Zaragoza), Palace garden, the fountain of tritons in Aranjuez, the Arch of Titus in Rome... He also painted

Francisco Pacheco, St. Pedro Nolasco Embarking, Provincial Museum of Fine Arts, Seville.

several still lives, keeping alive the unique and new spirit that his master gave to this kind of painting.

ALONSO CANO

The Granadine Alonso Cano, born in 1601, was a painter, sculptor and architect. Although his genius is most evident in drawing and sculpture, he has also left behind some remarkable canvases of striking formal beauty. In the year of 1652 he painted the ''Seven joys of the Virgin'' for the cathedral of Granada. Although his religious works (Virgins) obtained a great steem, he was also a fine painter of nudes,

as may be seen in the Descent to Hell, where we find some of the best anatomies found in Spanish Art.

LUIS MORALES

Luis Morales, also called ''the Divine,'' was born in Badajoz around the year 1500. He worked in accordance with the over-detailed techniques and methods originating from the medieval craft tradition, helped by his own family in the studio. He is one of the most inspired and fine painters of the mannerist tradition. The spirituality and refinement of his madonnas has no parallel

Antonio de Pereda, Life is a Dream, Real Academia de San Fernando, Madrid.

Antonio de Pereda, The Reinforcement of Genoa by the Second Marquis of Santa Cruz, The Prado, Madrid.

Mazo, Hunting at the "Tabladillo" in Aranjuez, The Prado, Madrid.

in the art of his time. The silky tones of his grays remind us of the mysterious brush of Leonardo.

He attained an undoubted mastership of his favorite themes: Ecce Homo and the Madonna with the Boy.

FRANCISCO DE HERRERA

Francisco de Herrera, called "the Older," because his son was also dedicated to painting, was born in Seville around 1576. He was a painter with great temperament, master of the free stroke and baroque feeling. All his paintings show real inspiration, whether he worked in the mannerist style or with his own instinctive vehemence. Though he was not an original artist, he painted numerous fine works for several religious institutions, such as La Pentecostés (the Whitsuntide), the Healing and Communion of San Buenaventura, Santa Ana with the Holy Family, the Pope San León 1st, and many more.

Alonso Cano, Madonna with Child, Monastery of the Escorial.

Luis Morales, Tryptych, Ecce Homo, and St. John of Ribera as a donor, Provincial Museum of Fine Arts, Cádiz.

FRANCISCO RIBALTA

The Catalonian Francisco Ribalta, born in 1565, worked in Madrid and Toledo with the best painters of his time, El Greco, Navarrete, and Sánchez Catán. From these masters he probably inherited his deep concern for the effects of light, which is manifested in one of his earliest works, the Crucified Christ, kept in the Hermitage. Ribalta moved to Valencia in 1599 under the protection of the archbishop Juan de Ribera, and in this city he painted some of his most beautiful works: the

Altar-piece of the Cartuja de Potaceli, the Last Supper, the Apparition of Christ to San Vicente Ferrer, etc.

MENENDEZ

Luis Eugenio Menéndez or Meléndez, was the descendant of a notable dynasty of Asturian painters who all worked in the Spanish court. He was born in Naples in 1716, and his first studies were carried out in his father's workshop. His fame

is mainly based on the forty-four still lives he painted between 1760 and 1772 for the Palace of Aranjuez. His contemporaries called him the ''Spanish Chardin.'' His works have less mystic strength than the famous still lives by Zurbarán, but he is a remarkable master of form and the sensual baroque line.

Index

Printed in Spain      GEOCOLOR®

M R - T M

Villa Sala Hnos.
Dep. Leg. B-75